Shaken To My Bones

A Poetic Midrash on the Torah

Brian Rohr

Teaneck, New Jersey

SHAKEN TO MY BONES © 2024 Brian Rohr. All rights reserved. No part of this book may be used or reproduced in any manner whatsoever without written permission except in the case of brief quotations embodied in critical articles and reviews.

Published by Ben Yehuda Press
122 Ayers Court #1B
Teaneck, NJ 07666

http://www.BenYehudaPress.com

To subscribe to our monthly book club and support independent Jewish publishing, visit https://www.patreon.com/BenYehudaPress

Jewish Poetry Project #44   http://jpoetry.us

Ben Yehuda Press books may be purchased at a discount by synagogues, book clubs, and other institutions buying in bulk. For information, please email markets@BenYehudaPress.com

"He Did Wild Things" first appeared in *The Jewish Literary Journal*, issue 120, (June 2023). jewishliteraryjournal.com.

Cover art: Zikaron Teruah by Yoram Raanan Learn more at YoramRaanan.com.
ISBN13: 978-1-963475-40-1 pb 978-1-963475-41-8 epub

Library of Congress Cataloging-in-Publication Data

24 25 26 / 10 9 8 7 6 5 4 3 2 1   20240811

This book is dedicated to my beautiful family
Sarah, Gabriel, and Charlie

It is also dedicated to a great teacher
Rabbi Aryeh Hirschfield, z"l
Without him, I may never have found my way back to Judaism.

Contents

Blessing

Calling Yaakov 3

Genesis / *Bereishit*

Bereishit Before 6
Noach A Second Life, Retold 7
Lech Lecha He Did Wild Things 9
Vayera My Longing 10
Chayei Sarah So Shall Be I 11
Toledot The Wild Hunter Scares You 12
Vayetzei Always, They Were Stories... Until 13
Vayishlach Echoes From Old Wounds 14
Vayeshev You are Blessed, Not Through the Love ... 15
Miketz The Darkness of the World Asks So Much From Us 17
Vayigash I am Joseph 19
Vayechi The Last Breath 20

Exodus / *Shemot*

Shemot Do You Not See That I Am Powerless By My Past? ... 24
Vaera If You Are Willing 25
Bo Some Days My Heart Too is Hardened 27
Beshalach Sometimes Liberation Comes to
   Those Not Yet Ready 28
Yitro They, Broken Down 29
Mishpatim When an Ox Has Gored Before 30
Terumah With Acacia Wood and Gold 31
Tezaveh The Only Appropriate Substance to Cleanse 32
Ki Tissa A Stone Whose Purpose Is Yet Unknown ... 33
Vayakhel In the Giving 34
Pekudei The Fire in the Cloud Has Returned 35

Leviticus / *Vayikra*

Vayikra A TV Commercial for Forgiveness: In Honor of God .. 38
Tzav Today, the Oil 39
Shemini Sometimes Things Are Just How They Are 40
Tazria The Affliction Struck, Again 41
Metzora And Crimson Stuff 42
Acharei Mot Off to the Wilderness for Azazel 43
Kedoshim Outside It Is Raining 44
Emor No Greater Betrayal 45
Behar To Return. Home. 46
Bechukotai Curiosity Can Soften the Heart of a Question 47

Numbers / *Bamidbar*

Bamidbar Take a Blue Cloth
   and Cover Each Part With Great Care 50
Naso A Common Problem That So Often Plagues 51
Beha'alotecha Their World Was Uprooted Once Again 52
Shelach Lecha God Must See Death Differently Than I 53
Korach Because a Vengeful God Makes Sense 54
Chukat For Miriam - In the Darkness They Cried Out 55
Balak Wisdom Finds Passion and Forms Into Action 56
Pinchas I Fear to Question 57
Mattot A Sign Upon My Door 58
Masei Sanctify for Me a City of Refuge 59

Deuteronomy / *Devarim*

Devarim Before We Enter, We Must Know Our History 62
Vaetchanan The Unspoken Song 63
Eikev But That Is Not What I See 65
R'eih Trouble Will Come, at Some Point 66
Shoftim "Raise for Me a Prophet," I Scream 67
Ki Tetzei In the Cool Air of the Morning Mist 69
Ki Tavo Olives and Grapes 70
Nitzavim Today I Returned 72
Vayelech Belief is Powerful, It Changes Us 73
Haazinu It Makes Me Wonder and Question Thus 75
Vezot HaBerachah When a Teacher Dies 77

Acknowledgements.. 79
About the Author.. 81

Blessing

Brian Rohr

Calling Yaakov

My father's uncle stood
      before me.

His smile, distant, gentle yes, though far
away, like seeing/not seeing through thick
gray clouds, a barrier of weather,
between me and my ancestors.

We share a sacred name, he and I.
Forged in the tongue of the ancient ones,
bestowed upon he, father of thirteen,
father of nations, a heel of a man
the stories say.
      Oh, what did I inherit?

I never knew him, Yaakov.
He died young yet steadies my footsteps
when I am called to approach the scroll.
Curious, open, even disturbed.
Hungry for meaning. Hungry for roots.

We become I/uncle/ancestor.
Merge into letters and sound,
trust in those who believe
names have meaning,
words have power, intention.

All together we dive headfirst into a stream of
answers and questions, undulating in a dance,
reaching for a glimpse of the divine.

I could be here forever.
I am in a room, within a book,
I am beside the Pacific Sea,
I am in a forest gathering fir cones.
I am studying the magnificence of creation.

I am here with my ancestors, ready.
      La'asok, b'divrei, Torah

Genesis

Bereishit

Bereishit

Before

Before
when waters were still
in the darkness
before the dream
did something stir?

A star shoots across the sky,
though there is no sky,
nor star.

I wonder about these moments,
though there isn't yet an I.

The untamed words have power.
The soon-to-be-song welcomes life.

A coming together until they coalesce,
a primal chaos sings

Let there be light…

…And there was.

Noach

A Second Life, Retold

The creative process is tricky.

A thought, an image, the way
her hand moves, brushing against
a bit of yellow fabric, against
a rough wall, can inspire a piece,
whole and understood.

Other times, it strains,
becoming a backbreaking,
soul crushing, slog,
to find the right words.
Ten thousand competing parts
nothing worth the time or salt.

God knows this, too.
Soon after the finest creation,
the planet, the sun, the sky,
plants and trees, fruit, animals, humans,
breathed into life, mud and dust.

But, it wasn't right. Wasn't satisfying.
And like a writer tossing incomplete
pages into the bin, half thoughts,
disappointed ideas,
God destroys this work to start fresh.

Yet there is often a line,
an idea that won't let go.
All artists know this.
That *thing* that longs to be carried over,
Fish swimming deep stories.
Birds flapping maps.
Comfort. Noach.

So when the world flooded
something new emerged,
which allowed for Abraham,
for Moses, which allowed for
something important, masterful.

Which allowed for you.

Majestic, in the place of the old.
Hinting, always hinting
to the wondrous possibility
of a second life, retold.

Lech Lecha

He Did Wild Things

Though not a wild man,
he did wild things,
upon hearing God's voice,
he considered it

a friend,
a partner.

Upon moving west,
  completing the journey
  his grief-stricken father could not,
he placed an altar,
and changed history.

He was a man with a knife.
Fear and trust surged through him
He had purpose.

Kings knew his name,
  knew Sarai.
Wealth was gained.

Kings too battled, defeated
for betraying his kin.

A wild ass born.

While counting stars,
on a cool clear night,
he grabbed a covenant
from the sky and fashioned
a knife for cutting the skin
of his people, of his son,
of his own, made sacred. Holy.

He, a man not wild,
He, a man who did wild things.

Vayera

My Longing

Blue and red birds appear in my birch tree,
squirrels run as I open the door.
They are charming, not my kin.

Truth is, I rarely welcome these days.

I long to open my tent like Abraham, the ancient one,
gather a choice kid, cook for a guest.
Offering up the most perfect grains,
fill the belly and heart, share music, truth.

I long for eyes and mouths,
words spun around the galaxy of a room.
Breathing the breath of a friend.

I long to dream wildly of angels bearing news.
Of cousins bearing news.

Years ago, in the before times
loved ones on the couch
or standing in the kitchen
told of pregnancy, of laughter,
of unbelievable events.

What is your message today? I hope to ask.
What bit of wisdom do you bring?

Between the stories of celebration and pain,
the holding of space, the counting of stars,
even between the longing, the answer,
as always, will be revealed.

Chayei Sarah

So Shall Be I

Will they someday write of my lineage
as a list that tells a deep rich history?
What will it say?
That my son, my favorite one, the one I love,
will have a life filled with stories and friendship?
With true love?

The ancient ones tell us
make sacred oaths with trustworthy
servants, to guarantee one's lineage.
I wonder, whom do I trust so much?
He who lusts, only pleasure of the eyes,
or he who prays with heart and cunning,
a talent for asking for signs from the divine?

The old storytellers say, look who feeds the camels
and offers strangers pure groundwater,
for the taste itself is 1000 spoken words.
And then if my trusted servant is awed, so shall be I.
So be I.

So, write my lineage as a story,
as verse, as a holy song.
Be brave enough to trust
and to love.

Toledot

The Wild Hunter Scares You

The wild hunter scares you,
admit it.

His hairy body, his gruff ways,
the lack of the civilized reminds you,
you do not know your way in the woods,
how to survive outside your front door,
beyond the bounds of the communal eruv.

He uses cunning
to trap the unsuspecting animal,

So you trick him,
using his hunger against him,
saying
        he must not be worthy.

But remember
your twin is you,
carrying what you don't.
The other. Two sides complete.

Yet, before you can reunite, you flee
for dishonoring your father, your brother.

You flee so you can live
and find the reason, remember the reason
for *teshuvah*, return, once again.

Vayetzei

Always, They Were Stories… Until

It was a story.
My grandfather told it as I sat by his bedside.
My father told it on nights when a fire burned in the hearth
and his heart was tender.
The story of their bond.
My grandfather would get clear eyed,
while my father would get a far-off gaze.
They experienced it differently.
Also differently than my mother,
she wasn't sure if it was a blessing or a curse.
But always, they were stories,
until deceit forced my hand and I left the abode,
alone, shivering, with only a rock for a pillow.
I woke up!
Now I too have been initiated
and it has left me, shaken,
shaken to my bones, in my soul.
to the very center of my being.
I know that I will never be the same, again.

Vayishlach

Echoes From Old Wounds

Echoes from old wounds,
rattle the bones of the hip,
a holy and sacred limping,
lest the patriarch forget.

Memories of deception,
　nowhere to flee
Seven times head lowered,
　feeling the earth.
Seven times wondering,
　would the sword strike?
　His head roll?

Instead they wrestle,
a game, falling on top of another,
a brotherly kiss,

almost they were joined back into one
the twins, separated at birth, betrayal.

So, cry those tears, o' brothers,
their rivers are the waters of *teshuva*,
we need them today, we need them today,
a secret fountain to drink from,
when hatred rises, fear divides,
and deception or error curses the land.

Cry those tears,
heal the future generations
who must battle that old wound over and over, again.

Let us bury our father together, holding hands,
so that we may finally say at the end of our days,
we did some good, and it was enough.

Vayeshev

You are Blessed, Not Through the Love

Having it all, except humility,
a mother, the acceptance you desire,
you walk through the world like a rainbow
shining a covenant that you cannot claim,
a covenant you cannot bestow.

Through garments and ditches dug deep
you release and arrive.
You are humbled lowly, each time testing you,
seeing if you are yet worthy of your lofted position:

The favorite son.
The head of your master's home.
And though a foreigner, even
in charge of a powerful land.

What are you wearing now?
What does it mean when garments
have been wrenched from your body?

Your positions are not you.
Others' views of you are not you.
Stop claiming this ridiculous claim,
for you are still leading your people to slavery.

Joseph, dear one, you are blessed,
not through love, but through your gifts.
You are a dream interpreter, an image reader,
a diviner, the veil is thin with you.
So, getting knocked is needed.
Getting humbled is right.

Because the moment we fully trust you,
as Joseph, as the one you are,
is when you are weeping on the neck of your father.

Seeing you cry reminds us of our own deepest longing.
Yet even then, your feet never fully touch the ground.
They never do, until your bones are carried
to the land of your fathers.

Miketz

The Darkness of the World Asks So Much From Us

It is solstice and warmth is a distant memory,
like fresh plums picked from the neighbor's tree.
This is the time when the sun stands still,
and the darkness of the world asks so much from us…

Slow down, remember.
Feel and reflect.

A time to honor the newly deceased
to remember our ancient ancestors.
A time for forgiveness.
A time for prayer.

—

Forgiveness.

I think of the stories of our people,
like when ten brothers bowed low,
asking for survival from the one they left for dead.

Oh, when they were recognized,
how the flood of hurt came back.
How the piercing of the veil of the past
mingled with the truths of the present.

Those dreams remembered are deep now.
Deeper than the pit he was offered to
like an unloved animal,
wounded in the heart.

And where the forgotten one now stands,
with the power to save nations,
will he be able to touch the 17-year-old of his past,
say to him, on the darkest day of the year,
today, is the day, we forgive?

Today
　is the day
　　we forgive.

And in doing so,
for family and the world,
call back the light.

Vayigash

I am Joseph

There are ways God speaks to me,
I can see it in my dreams,
and in the patterns of my life.

Like surrendering to some great river
whose destination is unknown
my feet and eyes are washed again
and I am used,
willfully and decisively.

It's no accident that brings you here,
brothers, no mere coincidence.
The struggles of our lives,
are twisted and intertwined,
crashing down together here and now.

I am Joseph, I scream to you,
I cry out after years, and my journey
finally leads to this understanding.

I am Joseph, I say,
as the salt of the ocean
streams down my face.

I am Joseph,
given a new name in this foreign land.

I am Joseph, and I ask
the only question that my heart,
now broken, can even consider
the only question that matters,

"Is my father still alive?"

Vayechi

The Last Breath

Twelve sons,
      each with a complicated past
      like your own complicated past,
      a knife thrown reckless and on target,
gather close without a sound,
your voice, weak.

Deathbed song, poem of blessing
assign fate, drive the future.

You see them, through them,
to an unmarked time,
highlighting qualities with vision,

unlike your father
whose own sight was fogged.

How do you write a poem about a poem,
live a life in the shadow of a life?

Break free

Jealousy
Politics
Fear
Regret
And joy
And grief
And revenge
And forgiveness

Arcing out to take hold, as the last breath is offered.
Tears fall in heaven. Tears fall in relief.

It is time to be carried to your people.
The ancestors welcome, invite you
to take a long and deserved rest.

Exodus

Shemot

Shemot

Do You Not See That I Am Powerless By My Past?

Humbled down, in murdering a man,
I changed my fortune and my worth.
For when my grandfather is set to kill me,
I wield stealthy justice, bade water to a family
whom the sacred has touched.

Now, I walk as if a veil lay between me and the land,
it was never truly my own. Removed from the riches,
I look like my ancestors, a shepherd, despised
by my Egyptian kin. This too feels right.
These days, there is not too much to say.

Then fire speaks, I am summoned.
Removing my shoes I feel, for the first time, holy ground.

What is this chore you ask of me?
I, who killed a man, and left him in the sand,
I, who have not even circumcised my son,
I, who do not know you,
don't you see that I am nothing,
powerless by my past?

Yet God grants me power *because* of my past.
I stumble my words, meant to move the tide.
I anger God by my protests.

So, to temper my heart, fear no mortal,
God sought my life in a nighttime journey.
Through the quick work of the priestess Zipporah,
my wife, did all of Israel get circumcised,
and with blood on the leg, saved.
For we were strangers in a foreign land.
Now, soon, we will be free.

Vaera

If You Are Willing

If you are willing, break away
from the noise, the literalists,
let in ancient mythic images,
so the real world can waken you open
and welcome you home.

The wild, ancient storyteller says
Listen up, open your heart's ears,
we are only three days deep.

Three days to unravel, unrestrict.
Three days to unwind.
Three days.

The prophet was not lying
when given the impossible task.
Those who can bear it, the fourth day
brings a conversation with God
a remembrance of the land.

What might be said, in those
secret words with the divine?

Take ownership back upon you,
find your soul deep in the forest,
rift with wolves, screeching owls.
Trying to be immortal hardens the heart,
only power, a pale substitute for love, remains.

Take ownership back upon you,
free the masses from your weak grip,
taste the nourishment of milk and barley.
When no pleasure remains, the crops
and beasts falter under your pride.

Take ownership back upon you,
authority not forced but something
the earth bestows, a depth of having walked
on holy ground, found when you
search within, not in your neighbor's yard.

Take ownership back upon you
while love and trust may betray, hate always will.
Hold strong the nighttime flight of your dream, returning to you
something beautiful, pure, a gift found in words
woven into the thread of life, saying

> no matter where you go,
> nor what you do, nor what you say,
> you can always go home,
> and find your true place,
> by traveling only three days deep.

Bo

Some Days My Heart Too is Hardened

Some days my heart too
is hardened. Locked shut,
no clear way out.

Mornings where an unkind word
from my beautiful son feels like an explosion,
grasping onto the momentous fear, discontent.

Those in power playing reckless games
with our lives.

Community condensed
into family units, condensed.
Singing through walls,
as air itself feels unsafe.
Masked and six feet across.

Removed. Below.

How many now? 500,000, 600,000,
1,000,000. First, second, third born.

It is enough to make me forget
that love, like God, is a verb,
needing tending.

Beshalach

Sometimes Liberation Comes to Those Not Yet Ready

The great separation occurred,
shaking the whole world awake.

Liberation forced with those not ready.
How could they be? They travel, needing food and water,
throats crying out in a wretched fear.

Shall we wait 400 more years for the brokenhearted?

It is not comfortable, nor pleasant, this freedom-making.
Back "home" it was a body owned and beaten,
yet there was food by the fire.

Here, by the water, there's nothing.
The bitterness stings.
This tenuous rebellion.

A piece of wood sweetens the water, however
– I love this – an herb relaxes them.
God relaxes them, for a moment.

> Your hearts are heavy, let me help you.
> Let me sweeten your bitterness,
> help you nourish your parched throats,
> and for a moment, relieve your burden.
> In doing so, remind you,
> that indeed you are not alone.
> You will be watched over you as you wander,
> wander through harsh and dry land.

Yitro

They, Broken Down

They,
broken down,
fearful and weathered,
distrusting as their children's fingerprints
still mark the bricks they left behind.

They,
not understanding
these new ways, this new God,
like their previous masters, though
more mighty and unknown.

They,
they cannot handle the power,
the words pierce their ears,
their eyes, confuse senses,
like birds with a shift
in the earth's magnetic fields,
unexplained.

They receive,
and they say yes.
Of course they say yes,
because truly,
what else would they say?
What else would they dare say?

Mishpatim

When an Ox Has Gored Before

When an ox has gored before,
there is God, waiting,
for we know what the ox is capable of,

And there is God teaching us that this *too* is sacred,
for it is community, and responsibility,
and powerful love.

The strongest of bonds,
that hold a people together,
even when trust has waned.

For the code is given as a divine mercy,
so that humans need not obsess,
nor disqualify another
by changing the laws at will.

So, the particulars of who pays what,
now can be seen, if one looks right,
      to the east, when the sun begins to rise,
as a love letter, from the One
who gifted the thousands of stars in the night sky,
to a people broken by the load on their back,
the memories of the stain of blood,
upon the weeping ground.

Terumah

With Acacia Wood and Gold

Carry me, with acacia wood and gold,
and reverence in your heart,
these laws I hold, ready to serve you.

I am a home, for the God whose fire
shown atop the mountain, confusing
senses, images fierce and unknown.

Materials gathered and gifted
those with and without gave,
made strong,
made strong.

These plans too are a gift.
The architect: All That Is
so you can remember,
to regard and hold true that

the boundaries of these walls,
give more freedom,
than alone, naked,
in the wilderness,

without a circle,
or a home.

Tezaveh

The Only Appropriate Substance to Cleanse

Today we sanctify the space.
beyond the realm of lust,
a space prepared in the appropriate ways

in the holiest of places,
a gateway of a thinning veil,
the waters of life inside a beast,
made sacred
the only appropriate substance to cleanse.

> (For those whom blood is taboo,
> never mind them,
> sex and death will always offend some.)

Blood, touching the altar
Blood, touching the ground
Blood, touching the side
Blood, touching the skin

Wild remembering,
life and death meet,
inviting God's breath,
to the most sacred place within,
the Holy of Holies,

like our own beating heart.

Ki Tissa

A Stone Whose Purpose Is Yet Unknown

There is a stone, whose purpose is yet unknown.
Unmoved for hundreds or even thousands of years,
now lifted and touched by human hands (maybe for the first time).

Carefully, in the light of the moon,
these hands tend to this stone, chiseling with great care,
working with love and reverence.

Symmetry is not needed, yet they must be perfect,
worked into two, these stones turn to tablets,
awaiting the word of God.

And the hands? They work knowing that soon,
the man they are attached to will change.
He must.

For hiding, he will see the Divine,
protected, and his face will be graced...
forever.

Vayakhel

In the Giving

They say the people danced
around their baby cow
their little god of gold.
Aaron made it, we all saw him do it.
No I didn't, Aaron said,
or, none of you are innocent.
None of us are innocent.

So when the call came,
it was time to give,
to give something of our own,
magnificent, something
sanctioned, ordered by the Divine,

it was a celebration of penance,
to make up,
and make beautiful.
       So,

We gave
We gave
We gave

The goat gave of its hair,
the dolphin of its skin.
We didn't regard the animals and trees,
we offered all we had, the last we had.
Obsessed with giving.

And in the giving,
some of us,
remembered how to love again.

And in the giving,
some of us
forgot how to dance.

Brian Rohr

Pekudei

The Fire in the Cloud Has Returned

Gazing at night upon that bright flame,
brings fear, yes, but a fear I can trust.
And so it brings a peace to aid my weariness.
For these days are long, and hard,
and it feels like yesterday, months really,
an eternity has passed, but who knows
what time is or what time it is, it feels like another life.

My soul hurts, I am proud, excited,
yet my soul feels contorted and broken.
I danced around that calf.

For when Moses left us, I could only guess if it was forever,
time had lost all meaning.
I danced, but my life was spared.
Some days I don't know right from wrong.

Yet there is hope on the horizon,
it seems we are moving toward some place
toward some land
that I don't even know how to long for.

But the fire in the cloud has returned,
I can see it, a guide I can surrender to,
trust, like a mother or a father,
in my generation.

Leviticus

Vayikra

Vayikra

A TV Commercial for Forgiveness: In Honor of God

Do you have guilt, blame, or shame?
Burn a cow, it's the name of the game.

Oh no, you made a mistake.
All you gotta do is burn a flat cake.

God loves a dash of salt,
Just don't put in any honey or malt.

The priest in his robes looks so fancy and clean,
A little blood on the ear, you know what I mean.

Is your lamb feeling a bit sick?
Don't bring it to the altar, God will see through that trick.

In the end, if you lie or steal,
Burn a ram to keep it real,

And return to the owner with an extra one fifth,
Wait and watch, God will forgive.

Tzav

Today, the Oil

The last of the oil drips,
baby green spinach anointed.
The preciousness of those final drops,
a virtually empty bottle.

How many olives pressed,
giving of the sun and the soil,
the rain and the wind,
in each passage over the lip
toward the bowl?

Don't dream too much.
Notice the richness.
Taste the spice.
There is flavor in the scarcity.
Delight in it.

Yet a new bottle awaits,
cracked open, the sound of the lid popping.
It is used, flowing, abundant.
Not drips, but pours, coating.

Preciousness in abundance.
Like Moses coating the tabernacle,
Aaron's head, preparing for the priesthood,
we consecrate a sacred meal,
spinach and basil, sun baked tomatoes,
delicate nasturtium seeds,
served with love and blessing.

We too believed this could last forever.

Shemini

Sometimes Things Are Just How They Are

Sometimes things are just how they are.
A tree grows from an acorn.
A fly lands on a half-eaten apple.
Fire consumes.

Grief, the feeling of loss is a celebration of life,
but sometimes there is no time to grieve,
for the tenuousness of life is still on the line.

This may infuriate,
but it is a cause and effect.
No different than an arrow shot in the air,
the need to land is not personal,
the need to land just is.

So if things are not prescribed,
at the greatest of heights,
when the doorway is open,
a God who had just consumed flesh
will continue to consume.

The ritual cannot stop, however.
The energies are invoked and
until they are contained,
a danger speaks out the words unsaid,
spoken by Aaron in his silence,
that this is real,
no doubt can be afforded,
nor any seriousness ignored.

Discernment,
with eyes unburdened,
by anything other than the dedicated task,
of seeing this through,
to the most awesome
and the most difficult end.

Tazria

The Affliction Struck, Again

Shame
   the priest is called
Responsibility
   the priest is called
Mingle
   the priest is called.

Our bodies are like clothing and walls,
mine is. Taken to the place that the impure go. Not
me, but it could be me. I would go

screaming to all who will listen,
   but almost everyone would turn away,
I usually do, shielding my eyes and children
from the wretched scene,
of that broken body.

I would disappear until all is made right.

When they return me, for it could be me,
my smooth skin would speak the words I couldn't speak.
I've see it on the faces of others who return,
about shame, about being betrayed
by that which can be no closer,
than the very surface of an unholy
and forever scarred body.

Metzora

And Crimson Stuff

What do I desire enough to please
the dirt and the trees, to please
the timbrels and the lyre?

Unblemished? Impossible.
Not interesting nor worthy the attempt.

Redemption, return from a great ordeal.
Healing, a wild ritual initiated.
ALIVE!
Blood sacrifice and crimson stuff,
cedar and hyssop.

Renewed, we can become an artist,
a poet, a tender of the land.

We can become a teacher.
We can become a friend.

Acharei Mot

Off to the Wilderness for Azazel

When no one knows who
or what Azazel is anymore,
we are lost in time,
in relations with the Earth.

Old words not valued,
old ideas not taught.
How do relationships even exist?

Azazel.
Azazel,
we stumble even at your existence.
Do you locate like Jerusalem, a place,
a sanctuary, the edge of a raging cliff?
Are you an old god, a demon,
breathing the Earth's dreaming?
What knowledge is held within you?

Tell me about rituals in the wild,
about long hair and horns.
What do you do with a goat
offered in your name?

Azazel.
I assume you know the worst.
That in our search for Hashem,
we betrayed the Earth,
the holy ground.

Kedoshim

Outside It Is Raining

and the trees are swaying with their gratitude.
The distance between my ancestors and me is far
both in land and in time. I ask, how
am I to understand the instructions they left me
when so much has happened and so much has changed?

A bird with a blue head and blue wings flies past my window
looking in, wondering why I am still inside
on such a day like today.

I too wonder about this and wonder if my ancestors
are standing behind me now, asking the same question.

Their world was so much different than mine. They spoke
for a divine energy in the voice of a masculine God,
whose notions of fair and unfair comfort, confuse and terrify.
Would my own lifestyle or beliefs ring of a defilement?

There is wisdom, for sure.
That which has carried my people far and wide.
The search for the holy, and to understand…
To understand the energy that permeates.

What vision can we therefore pick up,
when we, ourselves, are taught to both obey and wrestle?

No answers, only tension, like the sting of a harp,
a wildly played dulcimer, where the melody rings,
touching the familiar, and opening the heart,
the grief embedded in the questions:
Am I alive? And how have I lived my life?

Emor

No Greater Betrayal

My bones are broken, twisted,
my balls are crushed, and my fever runs high.

Who then, will look upon me for wisdom,
for leadership that the fearing God,
obsessed with purity, denies?

I do not want to be a priest, I do not desire to live
such a life. I do, however, want to be given
the dignity, to speak to God directly,
and to declare lepers impure, if I so choose.

They do let me eat of the first fruits and of
the sacred meat, I suppose I should be relieved.

But I am labeled in this priestly caste system,
labeled, yet I find the freedom to roam
and howl, and find my way among those others,
who are also cast aside, given new names.

And when the waters of the river touch my skin,
when I cleanse myself and breathe deep release,
it will be through my own code of purity that I
determine my worth. For I am forever marked,
and though I may walk among you, I will never be a part.

In that way, I am like all the others, awakened by
the indignity of judgment, because we humans know,
that any distinction will quickly turn to the unwanted,
unwelcomed, and the unloved.

For this, there is no greater betrayal.
For this, holds the gift, the possibility
of freedom.

Behar

To Return. Home.

Shema, Listen,
hear the sound of the ram's horn blow,
declaring the competition over.

Stop, notice,
let us dance naked in the wild fields,
gather without control.
Let us lay down our burdens,
see what the untended field yields.

It's a curiosity, wild trust.
Harder for some than others.
I wonder what it's like,
to return home,

to the land,

after all these years.
To return.
Home.

Bechukotai

Curiosity Can Soften the Heart of a Question

Over a conversation, sitting at the kitchen table,
the smell of freshly peeled oranges,
the young student observes
there are more curses than blessings.

She asks, *Why is that?*
And I have no good answer.

I do, however, invite the question to sit between us for a spell,
to take up space and join us for tea and orange slices.

We ask it other questions,
hoping to get to know it better.

What fears do you carry of your own?
What loves are you longing for?
If you could lay down your burdens,
how might you spend your time?

It was a good conversation all around,
and the sunlight slowly faded.

It was time to prepare dinner and say goodbye.
The young student thanked me,
saying, *That was an interesting thing,
learning how curiosity can soften the heart of a question,
and even the holiest of books
carry burdens we may never understand.*

I wiped my hands on a towel,
and thought, maybe we aren't being cursed after all,
just a recording of a world hurt by its own creation.

Numbers
Bamidbar

Bamidbar

Take a Blue Cloth and Cover Each Part With Great Care

There are parts inside each of us
that are so delicate
that great tenderness is needed.

Memories of your grandmother's baklava,
still warm in your hands,
the longing to taste them again, unfulfilled.

The scent of your mother's perfume
as she readies herself for an evening out.
That mix of excitement in the air.

Your father's tiredness after a long day's work.
The delight at seeing him, telling him partial stories
too fast for him to understand.

There are others as well,

your first secret love.
The nerves around that special kiss.
Seeing your child be born.

These parts can be spoken of casually,
of course, but this does a disservice.

Rather, we are told, take a blue cloth,
cover each part with great care.
When that is complete, wrap them with dolphin skin.
Let it be safe, let the most trusted carry them.

And when you do unwrap them,
their nostalgic comfort, make sure
that only the wise person is present,
lest the memories be desecrated and defiled
in the service of the mundane.

Brian Rohr

Naso

A Common Problem That So Often Plagues

Sometimes, when looking out the window, or reading a holy text,
I find that there is a common problem
that so often plagues culture and society.

To heal this cause, requires no less than the undoing of civilizations,
the rebuilding of the mind and heart.

Old patterns are rough, and the grooves in the road are deep,
but if we leave behind common transport for some simpler method,
we might slow down enough to walk toward a shared destiny.

And what is this that has wrought so much grief?

No more or less than man's belief
that he has the right and the power

to control women.

Beha'alotecha

Their World Was Uprooted Once Again

There is comfort in the known,
like seeing the weight of an apple on a tree,
we know it will bend the branch downward.

Or the predictability of coriander,
bursting on our tongue.

That's why we prepare so well
for the end of the world, or at least
for an earthquake, going over the instructions
a hundred times, the heady mingling
of excitement and stress, fear and possibility.

Like we read in the texts of our ancestors.
After a year of a life at the base of Sinai,
they left with new instructions, a new way.

After three days of journeying they arrive, pent up.
Needing to release the energy, they throw protest
upon the God who saved them. Of course they did,
their world was uprooted once again.

Moses asks God to take his life,
Miriam questions Moses's leadership,
Aaron finds displeasure.

Even God lacks patience.

It is like my own child as we prepare to move,
stubborn, obstinate and with physicality
he lashes out towards those he trusts.

And I, like God, send demerits,
rather than what was truly needed

a pause, a break, some love, an open heart
and time. Time to ground, to understand, to heal.

Shelach Lecha

God Must See Death Differently Than I

From the perspective of *Ain Sof*, what does my life mean?
Just dust and mud, breath separating me from the holy earth.

When the fear of the multitudes reached the ears of the divine,
a plague was offered, a genocide, reversed only because
reputation matters. This divine being, full of compassion
and full of anger.

This is the God I can wrestle with,
on dark days and into the night.

In my heart, however, this is not the God I pray to.
I use different metaphors that speak to me
of a more mysterious universe.
Of possibilities I cannot comprehend,
of motivations, I can never know,
but clues are dropped
and I can search those like a detective,
on a quest for something more beautiful,
holy and full of awe.

And of the man,
who was stoned by God's own hand,
working through the anger of the people?

Let us hold him now, as a sacrifice,
to a remembering of a time,
maybe even still to come,
when rather than a threat,

some warm broth and a soothing song
can help us on our sacred journey
reminding us of the direction home.

Korach

Because a Vengeful God Makes Sense

Maybe it is simple. I don't know
what it means to erase a family.
How do we explain it to the children?
Or the children's children?

Swallowed, consumed, yet not dead.
What's it like to live in some underworld—
do they feel us, all that weight?

This brings up deeper questions…
Why would someone even write this story?
Who would want such a vengeful god?

But maybe the questions are wrong.

Sacred stories don't arise out of desire,
at least not the good ones. Rather, they
explain a reality, understanding an earthquake
can never be just the movement of land
not for those who can feel the subtlety
of all that is around them.

No, there must be a vengeful god,
because a vengeful god makes sense.
More sense than a void. More sense
than no meaning and lost alone
in time and space, forever.

Chukat

For Miriam - In the Darkness They Cried Out

"Miriam, Miriam…"
And where she had once answered,
There was silence.

"Miriam?" They cried,
it was Rosh Chodesh
and the women were the first to realize,
the loss of their prophetess, their teacher.

Worry filled their hearts.
They knew their destiny,
they had seen the death amongst their kin,
yet this was different,
it was Miriam, it made their fate more real.

Miriam, Dancer,
Protector, Water-Diviner,
Keeper of the Ancient Stories.

Miriam,
we are without you,
and we are scared.

Balak

Wisdom Finds Passion and Forms Into Action

This man is not crazy,
he knows both kings and holiness.

He is not crazy, but the times he lives in are.

There's a donkey who stumbles,
and speaks: "What have I done…?"

This man's loyalty is not to the ragged band below.
An angel confronts this Destroyer of People,
as a reminder where true loyalty stands.

But if we look closer
we see a break, dissidence,
the blessing rains down from the cliffs above,
towards a rebellious people
uninterested in their God.

These people are not blessed because of an inherent goodness.
This is a lesson that needs to be shouted out.
It is not a piety that earns them favor.
They are blessed and chosen because they *are*.
Because of promises made long ago.

Because of the bones they carry and his ancestors.

For wisdom finds passion, and forms into action.
As once, Abraham looked to the stars,
and found his joy,
he left his home and opened his tent.
It coincided with a friend in All That Is,
who promised to watch over his lineage
until the end,
til the very end.

Pinchas

I Fear to Question

We are nearing the end of the journey.
The land is so close, we can smell the date trees.
The hints of giants died along with our fathers.

Our numbers have been purged,
the unfaithful weeded out,
so that a new generation,
who exacts correct loyalty,
can be given the gift of home.

I fear to question.
For questioning brings dire consequences.
Yet in my heart I wonder…

This God, proclaimed as fair, yet my own eyes
witness a different reality, a different proof.

Women denied true agency.
Death freely given to disagreers.
The land promised is full of inhabitants.

So I question in my heart only,
for my sons must be allowed to grow and choose,
have the opportunity to right the wrongs
that our ancient ones thought reasonable and fair.

And some day, in the first month, when the moon
is full of potential and light, we will tell the story,
expanded, to include the fight for justice,
for freedom, for dignity, for all.

And when the seventh moon begins,
we shall hear the sound of the ram's horn,
blown into the air, a reverberating sound
a song for all people… a song of freedom.

Mattot

A Sign Upon My Door

The sign on my door says "closed" –
I am busy taking inventory
of the things that help me breathe,
that keep me from sleep.

What promises made
long ago still play on the record
in the room no one enters?

I am used to the faint sound,
but forget the purpose.

Were they vows made to myself?
To others? To God?

Can I nullify in the name of my pain?

Today I am a man.
Today I am a daughter in my father's house.
Today I am a woman recently married.
Today I am widowed.
Today I am divorced.

Can I cry out *Kol Nidre* in the name of my pain?
Will this free me of all that lingers?

Tonight I am closed.
Tomorrow open me up,
bring me back to community
bring me back
       to love.

Masei

Sanctify for Me a City of Refuge

Sanctify for me a city of refuge
where I can go
when the ugly news
and the harsh things
break me
and my innocence is shattered.

Sanctify for me a city of refuge
that I can enter when
I speak, unknowingly,
and escape the thoughts
my mind meant as secret.

Sanctify for me a city of refuge
where I can go when I,
like the actor,
kill a woman with a gun
not intended to kill
and I am terrified at what I have done,
and confused.

Sanctified for me a city of refuge
where I can go
where anyone can go
when they are fearful
or hungry
or tired.

Sanctify for me a city of refuge
that won't close its doors
on the immigrant
that won't close its doors
on the Muslims
that won't close its doors
on the Jews
that won't close its doors.

Sanctify for me a city of refuge
for anyone who needs
a city of refuge.

Sanctify for me
in Brazil,
Afghanistan,
Turkey,
Poland,
Ethiopia,
the United States,
Haiti,
Saudi Arabia,
a city of refuge
where one can walk down the street
regardless of their gender
their race,
their sexuality,
their fashion style,
their disability,
or their beliefs.

Sanctify for me a city of refuge,
where you,
God,
can sanctify
me.

Sanctify for me
a city
    of refuge.

Deuteronomy
Devarim

Devarim

Before We Enter, We Must Know Our History

We must learn how our fathers, our brothers,
our uncles missed the mark so terribly.
How their lives became synonymous with
fault and betrayal.

Today, we will take up the mantle.
There are no elder men, save for three.

I am a fortunate one. Before my father died of
the plague he taught me the skills needed to
live a life. Shared his values, told me of his parents.

He saw the death of his friends,
knowing what was to come.

Today, our leader tells us of their failures,
bickering masses, fearful spies. I don't remember
much about *Mitzrayim*. About that narrow space
where we had no agency, no freedom, no dignity.

What I know is that it has been hard
for my people. Hard to enter a new possibility.
Maybe that is how anyone would be. Possibly.

But soon, I will tend to the land, and know
that land as mine and my clan's, and my people's.
Or so the Divine has promised.

Tonight, however, I will listen, by the fire,
of the struggles my people experienced,
to prepare me to enter the land,
ready and adorned.

Vaetchanan

The Unspoken Song

a holy pain, threatens to rip my chest.

I address you, the masses, the so-called
chosen ones, and it is with an imploring voice,
for my own fate is hard to accept.

It is not about me anymore, nor was it ever,
but now, truly, you can see that it is about you
and God. You are about to enter a place
that was never meant for me.

I was used, and I accept that,
in fact, I've even reveled in it, because
I thought my reward would be the land,
to touch the earth that Jacob touched,

Yaakov, he wrestled, and was rewarded.

Abraham, he journeyed and obeyed…
and was rewarded.

And what is my reward? I am Moses,
the great leader, written about for ages,
yet for me it was never about my posterity.
        It was the land that called to me.

She whispered to me in my dreams,
I could still see her upon my waking.

But my vision is clear now, from up here,
on top of the summit. The directions tell me
a story of our past and our future.

I was used, but you need to see that I am
not your god, nor your hero. I am Moses.
Only Moses. The one drawn from water to
help you in the desert. The one to hold
you and support you in the in-between place.
The *mezuzah*. The mandorla. The threshold.
The journey of ten thousand steps. Bringing you
to this boundary, to see your destiny.

Were I to enter with you, it would be about me.
You would make me king, and in doing so, you
would never know yourselves, see that destiny flourish.

I was never meant to enter, this was the plan
from the start. I can see it more clearly now,
the pain does not lessen by knowing this,
but there is poetry and song in it. A dirge that
moves the heart and shakes the soul.

Knowing this too, gives an urgency. My brother
and sister are dead, as are many of your beloved.
My time is up.

So heed these words, *Shema*. Listen. Behold. Remember.
And learn to speak with the holy divine,
a fire that can quench any thirst.

But to myself, my own song sings.

To touch the land would have been nice, though.
Ah, to just touch the land.

Eikev

But That Is Not What I See

I once had a dream. I was riding on a train through a land I had not previously known. We were nearing a tunnel, burrowed through a mountain. A large sign welcomed the train, proclaiming, *The Land Of Milk And Honey – Your Ancestors Are Buried Here*. Was this the cave Abraham once purchased? Was this the land my people knew?

I turned to look at the other passengers, and rather than joy, there was a look of fear, and concern. The tunnel was dark, and the passengers spoke:

"I have provoked the Lord by working on Shabbat." Another said, "I thought the miracles at Egypt were just a made-up fiction." Another said, "I have sinned and worshiped the Torah scroll like an idol."

"The milk is not milk," I thought, "but the fear passed from parent to child. The honey is not honey, but the punishment that sticks through millennia." And now I understand the death of Moses to have been a betrayal for us all, for now, he cannot intercede on our behalf as he once did for the people, and for Aaron. We are truly alone.

We emerge out of the cave and I expect to see fire and brimstone, blood in the river, scarred trees. But that is not what I see. Instead, there are 10,000 birds in the sky circling over the fields, singing a song that shakes my bones, and I realize that this really is the land of my ancestors. I am home.

R'eih

Trouble Will Come, at Some Point

Maybe between the falling
of leaves and their budding,
or when the rains fail,
trouble will come, to you, or your spouse,
your children or their children, trouble will come,
and help will not be provided from within.

An inevitable reality, though
when pride and guilt commingle
asking is hard, but you must
and the community will oblige.

You will be held.

When your debt is too great
to pay off in a lifetime, there
is an end, for in the seventh year
your burden will be lifted.

A society structured to
serve the people, for trouble will come
at some point, and what a thing,
when society itself is ready to catch you.

Shoftim

"Raise for Me a Prophet," I Scream

I read the news.
Another tragedy.
Another betrayal.

The planet is dying,
our technology faulty.

My heart burns with a fire,
no perfect ox exists.
No offering can be made.

Who then,
if we cannot speak to the dead?

"Raise for me a prophet,"
I scream out.
Instead you send a con man.

We are lost and hurting.

"Raise for me a king."
Instead you send a dictator,
who has no idea how to read or write.

This is not Sodom,
America, but we must reckon.
For though the prophecy did not come true,
the false prophet did not die
and no one is home in the city of refuge.

The trees remain,
however,
and I will hold onto them,
for the peaches and nectarines,
for the cherries,
and the tender, tender plums.

Ki Tetzei

In the Cool Air of the Morning Mist

we can see the breath,
strong but showing signs of wear.

The light, however, that shines off the face
is so bright, yet somehow easier to look at.

We don't need a veil anymore.

We are getting close,
the wood pile is getting smaller
and we are more discerning with what we use.
No one is collecting anymore.

We are all attentive, listening.
The elder is sharing his wisdom.
It has a rushed feeling,
as if there is more to tell than time allows.

He wants the best for us.
I feel that, trying to help instill a just society.
One that he cannot enforce.
And I wonder if he ever really knew us.

He is a man holding on longer,
but our beginning is his end,
and there is no doubt,
watching him share our story,
that this, truly,
is for the very last time.

Ki Tavo

Olives and Grapes

Olives and grapes.
Luscious berries on a prickly vine.
Pears ripe with juices that flow down the chin,
the children smile, as do adults, who indulge in its sweetness.

These fruits are the work of the soil and the plants.
Water and sun.
Insects and humans.
The earth and God.

And the first taste when the sun turns warm against the skin,
is like heaven, exploding on the tongue.

The first that grow however,
are not meant for consumption in the field,
nor on the family plate,
but reserved for a ceremony honoring the harvest,
honoring the divine in all.
For the water and soil and earth are not the Divine,
rather the Divine is the water and soil and earth.
And so much more.
Do you see the difference?

To give of the first fruits,
to truly give it over, in selfless homage,
calls forth a trust that more will come.
That the abundance will persist for another year.

When the dew sweetens the air with moisture in the morning,
and the grass wettens the feet,
and the dawn sun celebrates its light upon the land,
the holy work commences,
the carefully woven baskets collect
what the hands have picked,

what the insects have pollinated,
what the plant has grown,
what the water and soil nourished,
what the earth has provided,
what God has infused with life.
And that is the blessing,
and all, all is good.

Nitzavim

Today I Returned

Today I returned from walking the neighborhood with my son and his friend, exploring the flowers and trees and tomatoes, grown in the late summer gardens. Along the way, we met a woman, 96 years old, who was bent over in her yard, pulling up a weed. It had invaded her daffodils.

She told us of the town where she grew up on the east side of the state. A small logging town with two rows of houses, it has since been torn down with a park put in its place. I think of this as I return once again to the cycle, celebrating the creation of the world, a new year.

In the beginning the world was so full of promise. But we were made in God's image, a warning shot through the ages.

And traveling, still traveling, when we get to where we are going, finally, returning to the land where our ancestors dwelt, we are told we shall bow to no other, no idol, for to God that is adultery. If we do, if we succumb to that most disgraced of acts, we will be plucked from the garden like an unsavory weed invading the preciousness of the daffodils. We will be torn down so something more faithful can reside in our place.

Vayelech

Belief is Powerful, It Changes Us

Belief is powerful.
It changes us.

Resting between light and dark,
an unknown thought creeps in,
too small to even notice,
but it touches a part that has been
lying dormant for one thousand years.
God can see it, for the microscopic eyes
are looking for betrayal, always looking for betrayal,
God's greatest fear.

And in that space,
without even needing to see true future,
an understanding sets in about the nature
of those who long for connection.

It is easier to be loyal to one god.
It is hard to *believe* in one god.
To believe, even with the miracles,
that there are no more than this.
The diversity of the world laughs.

But there is a unity that connects all,
a force that binds the intent to light,
to energy, to form, to life.
It is hard to see without a city like Jerusalem,
inside the gates one can feel it, and speak of it.

But even those who reside there have rarely touched it.
Moses did, for a brief moment,
and his face was never the same.

But it is hard.

And God sees the seed of doubt, the desire
for the multitude. Instead of a courtship, however,
at this late date, the Divine proclaims disappointment,
using verse as witness, to hide away.

Moses was 120 years old,
and he sacrificed so much.
What else would he do?
Stay a shepherd on his wife's father's land?

Instead, he journeyed and fell in love with God,
and tried with his heart and words to give meaning.

To be the mediary who says
there is truly only One,
now go and believe.

Haazinu

It Makes Me Wonder and Question Thus

Yellow edged leaves, the first of autumn
a school bus driving by,
covered with early morning condensation.

How do you think of yourself
when great change is coming?
What is your composure?

The teachers say to take extra time,
and gentleness.
Though it is not advice easily taken.

Rather, transitions bring great emotions,
amongst humans and amongst God.

For in a beginning, there was an idea, to create,
and full of awesome power, a new world was born.

The relationship with individuals
was something to behold.
Noah, Abraham, Jacob, Moses.
There seemed to be true regard, even love.

But oaths were made,
and oaths are powerful things.

To never destroy the world again.
To watch over the descendants.
To make them as numerous as the stars.
The promises of land.

Now, however, on the eve of fulfillment,
questions burn, asked without pity,
but in stark relief, for final messages speak truth,
and in the last before we enter the new land,
God throws forth fierce words
rendered within a poem, to be remembered.

It makes me wonder and question thus:
Does God even like us?

And does God regret the oaths once made?

Vezot HaBerachah

When a Teacher Dies

When a teacher dies, birds fly askew,
temples sink and poets pause…

Out in the wilderness the mountaintops moan,
the goats sigh, and the Douglas Firs mourn
as if he were one of their own.

Sentimentality has no place.
  It has no place.
No words can console,
  nor should they.

I think of Danny, and Aryeh.
I think of Zalman. I think of Moses.

I think of their teachers, and of pottery
broken on the ground.

The world is *not* perfect because it has death.
The world is *more* perfect because it has death.

We grieve, heap praise upon the dead,
there is no greater honor. Black cloth
ripped, our shirts, ripped, the dirt
upon our face becomes mud.

When a teacher dies, the world stops.
And then we move on,
forced to be greater
       than we ever were.

Acknowledgements

Commitments are powerful things, like a covenant. They can protect life and forge bonds, they can even create a book.

It was October 2020, the beginning of 5781, when I made the stretch and commitment to read the entire Torah, something that as a Jewish adult - and a Jewish storyteller - I hadn't fully ever done. It was an interesting time. The world was about seven months into a global pandemic, we had just had the first "virtual" High Holy Days, and it was rare to see someone in the community in-person. Sometimes going out of the house felt dangerous. It is hard to remember that now.

I had signed up for a Torah study class to help me in my stretch. Prior to the first session, I wrote a poem on *Bereishit*. I read it during that first class, and it got a good response. So, I wrote another poem the second week, and one for the third. At that point, I noticed what I was doing, so I made a commitment to myself - to write a poem each week based on the weekly *parshiyot*/Torah portion for the whole year. It was a rich and meaningful practice. Through this process, I was able to wrestle with the text, examine it, and have a creative way to explore my ideas and reactions. It is something anyone can do. I invite you to give it a try.

When the year was up, looking back at the poems I had written, I realized that I had something unique, something I hadn't planned on. I had a poetry manuscript.

I want to thank Rabbi Eve Posen and all of my classmates in my Torah study class who received my poems each week, encouraged me, and allowed the poems to bring our conversations deeper. Honestly without you all, this book wouldn't exist.

I want to thank Rabbi Dan and Zoë Goldblatt, Tivona Reith, and Sheila Bender as early readers who gave me solid feedback and advice.

I am eternally grateful to the fabulous writer/poet Marcela Sulak whose expertise, notes, and feedback helped turn a rough draft into something worth sending out.

I am grateful to Ellen Goldblatt who provided me with encouragement at a time when I might have given up.

I am so thankful to Larry Yudelson of Ben Yehuda Press for being a great partner in publishing this book, and to Julia Knobloch, the poetry editor of BYP who saw something in this manuscript and helped me fine tune it to bring it to completion.

To my parents and brother who always have encouraged my pursuit of the arts, and instilled in me that a creative path in life is worth it.

And of course, without a doubt, I want to thank my beloved partner Sarah who has seen me grow as a writer, who has rooted me and rooted for me, and been the source of many love poems (maybe another book?). She, along with our son Gabriel - a budding writer in his own right - would excitedly ask to hear the poems each week. Both of their support was what I needed to keep me going. My youngest son Charlie wasn't born when I wrote most of them, but screamed with joy along with the rest of the family when I shared the news that my book was accepted to be published! You three guide me and remind me of what is important. Thank you.

About the Author

Brian Rohr is a poet and performative storyteller, residing in the Pacific Northwest. His work has been featured in the *Jewish Literary Journal* and *Blink Ink*, and his essay, "On Being a Story-Carrier" was published in the two-volume book set about Jewish Storytelling, *P'ri Etz Yitzhak, Fruit of Yitzhak's Tree*. He is the founder and director of The Stafford Challenge, an international poetry project inspiring over one thousand participants to write a poem every day for a year, influenced by the legendary poet William Stafford. As a storyteller, Rohr has taught and performed at major conferences, high schools, universities, synagogues, libraries, and solo concerts. He is a proud father and husband and loves green and herbal teas. Learn more at brianrohr.com.

The Jewish Poetry Project

jpoetry.us

Ben Yehuda Press

From the Coffee House of Jewish Dreamers: Poems of Wonder and Wandering and the Weekly Torah Portion by Isidore Century

"Isidore Century is a wonderful poet. His poems are funny, deeply observed, without pretension." —*The Jewish Week*

The House at the Center of the World: Poetic Midrash on Sacred Space by Abe Mezrich

"Direct and accessible, Mezrich's midrashic poems often tease profound meaning out of his chosen Torah texts. These poems remind us that our Creator is forgiving, that the spiritual and physical can inform one another, and that the supernatural can be carried into the everyday."
—Yehoshua November, author of *God's Optimism*

we who desire: Poems and Torah riffs by Sue Swartz

"Sue Swartz does magnificent acrobatics with the Torah. She takes the English that's become staid and boring, and adds something that's new and strange and exciting. These are poems that leave a taste in your mouth, and you walk away from them thinking, what did I just read? Oh, yeah. It's the Bible."
—Matthue Roth, author of *Yom Kippur A Go-Go*

Open My Lips: Prayers and Poems by Rachel Barenblat

"Barenblat's God is a personal God—one who lets her cry on His shoulder, and who rocks her like a colicky baby. These poems bridge the gap between the ineffable and the human. This collection will bring comfort to those with a religion of their own, as well as those seeking a relationship with some kind of higher power."
—Satya Robyn, author of *The Most Beautiful Thing*

Words for Blessing the World: Poems in Hebrew and English by Herbert J. Levine

"These writings express a profoundly earth-based theology in a language that is clear and comprehensible. These are works to study and learn from."
—Rodger Kamenetz, author of *The Jew in the Lotus*

Shiva Moon: Poems by Maxine Silverman

"The poems, deeply felt, are spare, spoken in a quiet but compelling voice, as if we were listening in to her inner life. This book is a precious record of the transformation saying Kaddish can bring."
—Howard Schwartz, author of *The Library of Dreams*

is: heretical Jewish blessings and poems by Yaakov Moshe (Jay Michaelson)

"Finally, Torah that speaks to and through the lives we are actually living: expanding the tent of holiness to embrace what has been cast out, elevating what has been kept down, advancing what has been held back, reveling in questions, revealing contradictions."
—Eden Pearlstein, aka eprhyme

Texts to the Holy: Poems
by Rachel Barenblat

"These poems are remarkable, radiating a love of God that is full bodied, innocent, raw, pulsating, hot, drunk. I can hardly fathom their faith but am grateful for the vistas they open. I will sit with them, and invite you to do the same."
—Merle Feld, author of *A Spiritual Life*

The Sabbath Bee: Love Songs to Shabbat
by Wilhelmina Gottschalk

"Torah, say our sages, has seventy faces. As these prose poems reveal, so too does Shabbat. Here we meet Shabbat as familiar housemate, as the child whose presence transforms a family, as a spreading tree, as an annoying friend who insists on being celebrated, as a woman, as a man, as a bee, as the ocean."
—Rachel Barenblat, author of *The Velveteen Rabbi's Haggadah*

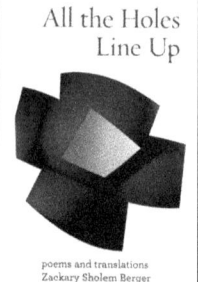

All the Holes Line Up: Poems and Translations
by Zackary Sholem Berger

"Spare and precise, Berger's poems gaze unflinchingly at—but also celebrate—human imperfection in its many forms. And what a delight that Berger also includes in this collection a handful of his resonant translations of some of the great Yiddish poets." —Yehoshua November, author of *God's Optimism* and *Two World Exist*

How to Bless the New Moon:
Songs of the Sovereign and the Icon
by Rachel Kann

"Rachel Kann is a master wordsmith. Her poems are rich in content, packed with life's wisdom and imbued with soul. May this collection of her work enable more of the world to enjoy her offerings."
—Sarah Yehudit Schneider, author of *You Are What You Hate* and *Kabbalistic Writings on the Nature of Masculine and Feminine*

Into My Garden
by David Caplan

"The beauty of Caplan's book is that it is not polemical. It does not set out to win an argument or ask you whether you've put your tefillin on today. These gentle poems invite the reader into one person's profound, ambiguous religious experience."
— *The Jewish Review of Books*

Between the Mountain and the Land is the Lesson: Poetic Midrash on Sacred Community
by Abe Mezrich

"Abe Mezrich cuts straight back to the roots of the Midrashic tradition, sermonizing as a poet, rather than idealogue. Best of all, Abe knows how to ask questions and avoid the obvious answers."
—Jake Marmer, author of *Jazz Talmud*

NOKADDISH: Poems in the Void
by Hanoch Guy Kaner

"A subversive, midrashic play with meanings—specifically Jewish meanings, and then the reversal and negation of these meanings."
—Robert G. Margolis

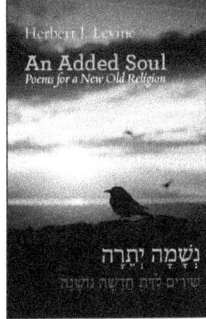

An Added Soul: Poems for a New Old Religion
by Herbert J. Levine

"Herbert J. Levine's lovely poems swing wide the double doors of English and Hebrew and open on the awe of being. Clear and direct, at ease in both tongues, these lyrics embrace a holiness unyoked from myth and theistic searching."
—Lynn Levin, author, *The Minor Virtues*

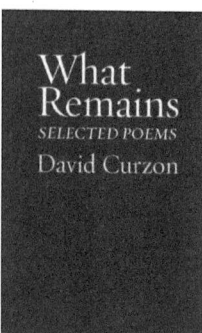

What Remains
by David Curzon

"Aphoristic, ekphrastic, and precise revelations animate WHAT REMAINS. In his stunning rewriting of Psalm 1 and other biblical passages, Curzon shows himself to be a fabricator, a collector, and an heir to the literature, arts, and wisdom traditions of the planet."
—Alicia Ostriker, author of *The Volcano and After*

The Shortest Skirt in Shul
by Sass Oron

"These poems exuberantly explore gender, Torah, the masks we wear, and the way our bodies (and the ways we wear them) at once threaten stable narratives, and offer the kind of liberation that saves our lives."
—Alicia Jo Rabins, author of *Divinity School*, composer of *Girls In Trouble*

Walking Triptychs
by Ilya Gutner

These are poems from when I walked about Shanghai and thought about the meaning of the Holocaust.

Book of Failed Salvation
by Julia Knobloch

"These beautiful poems express a tender longing for spiritual, physical, and emotional connection. They detail a life in movement—across distances, faith, love, and doubt."
—David Caplan, author of *Into My Garden*

Daily Blessings: Poems on Tractate Berakhot
by Hillel Broder

"Hillel Broder does not just write poetry about the Talmud; he also draws out the Talmud's poetry, finding lyricism amidst legality and re-setting the Talmud's rich images like precious gems in end-stopped lines of verse."
—Ilana Kurshan, author of *If All the Seas Were Ink*

The Missing Jew: Poems 1976-2022
by Rodger Kamenetz

"How does Rodger Kamenetz manage to have so singular a voice and at the same time precisely encapsulate the world view of an entire generation (also mine) of text-hungry American Jews born in the middle of the twentieth century?"
—Jacqueline Osherow, author of *Ultimatum from Paradise* and *My Lookalike at the Krishna Temple: Poems*

The Red Door: A dark fairy tale told in poems
by Shawn C. Harris

"THE RED DOOR, like its poet author Shawn C. Harris, transcends genres and identities. It is an exploration in crossing worlds. It brings together poetry and story telling, imagery and life events, spirit and body, the real and the fantastic, Jewish past and Jewish present, to spin one tale."
—Einat Wilf, author of *The War of Return*

The Matter of Families
by Robert H. Deluty

"Robert Deluty's career-spanning collection of New and Selected poems captures the essence of his work: the power of love, joy, and connection, all tied together with the poet's glorious sense of humor. This book is Deluty's masterpiece."
—Richard M. Berlin, M.D., author of *Freud on My Couch*

The Five Books of Limericks
by Rhonda Rosenheck

"A biblical commentary that is truly unique. Each chapter of the Torah is distilled into its own limerick, leading the reader to reconsider the meaning of the original text, and opening avenues for interpretation that are both fun and insightful."
—Rabbi Hillel Norry

Bits and Pieces
by Edward Pomerantz

"A stunning tapestry of family life in the 40s and 50s. Like all great poetry, Pomerantz's work expands after reading. Each poem is exquisitely structured, often with a stunning ending, into a masterful whole."
—Alan Ziegler, editor of SHORT: An International Anthology

Words for a Dazzling Firmament: Poems/Readings on Bereishit Through Shemot
by Abe Mezrich

"Mezrich is a cultivated craftsman— interpretively astute, sonically deliberate, and spiritually cunning."
—Zohar Atkins, author of Nineveh

Everything Thaws
by R. B. Lemberg

"Full of glacier-sharp truths, and moments revealed between words like bodies beneath melting permafrost. As it becomes increasingly plain how deeply our world is shaped by war and climate change and grief and anger, articulating that shape feels urgent and necessary and painful and healing."
—Ruthanna Emrys, author of A Half-Built Garden

Ode to the Dove
An illustrated, bilingual edition of a Yiddish poem by Abraham Sutzkever
Zackary Sholem Berger, translator
Liora Ostroff, Illustrator

"An elegant volume for lovers of poetry."
—Justin Cammy, translator of *Sutzkever, From the Vilna Ghetto to Nuremberg: Memoir and Testimony*

Poems for a Cartoon Mouse
by Andrew Burt

"Andrew Burt's poetry magnifies the vanishingly small line between danger and safety. This collection asks whether order is an illusion that veils chaos, or vice-versa, juxtaposing images from the Bible with animated films."
—Ari Shapiro, host of NPR's *All Things Considered*

Old Shul
by Pinny Bulman

"Nostalgia gives way to a tender theology, a softly chuckling illumination from within the heart of/as a beautiful, broken sanctuary, somehow both gritty and fragile, grimy and iridescent – not unlike faith itself."
—Jake Marmer, author of *Cosmic Diaspora*

Feet In L.A., But My Womb Lives In Jerusalem, My Breath In Vermont
by Lori Levy

"Reading through Lori Levy's new book of poems takes my breath away. With no pretense whatsoever, they leap, alive, from the page until this reader felt as if she were living Levy's life. How does the author do it?"
—Mary Jo Balistreri, author of *Still*

www.ingramcontent.com/pod-product-compliance
Lightning Source LLC
LaVergne TN
LVHW041342080426
835512LV00006B/583